the SCIENCE beHIND

THEME PARKS, PLAYGROUNDS AND TOYS

Nicolas Brasch

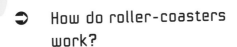

- How do roller-coasters work?

- Why do I look so silly in fairground mirrors?

- Do heavier people go down slides faster than lighter people?

MACMILLAN
LIBRARY

First published in 2010 by
MACMILLAN EDUCATION AUSTRALIA PTY LTD
15–19 Claremont Street, South Yarra 3141

Reprinted 2011

Visit our website at www.macmillan.com.au or go directly to www.macmillanlibrary.com.au

Associated companies and representatives throughout the world.

National Library of Australia Cataloguing-in-Publication entry

Brasch, Nicolas, 1961–
    Theme parks, playgrounds and toys / Nicolas Brasch.
    ISBN: 9781420268942 (hbk.)
    Brasch, Nicolas, 1961– Science behind.
    Includes index.
    For primary school age.
    Physical sciences—Juvenile literature.
530

Publisher: Carmel Heron
Managing Editor: Vanessa Lanaway
Editor: Georgina Garner
Proofreader: Kylie Cockle
Designer: Stella Vassiliou
Page layout: Stella Vassiliou and Raul Diche
Photo researcher: Sarah Johnson
Illustrators: Alan Laver, pp. 7, 17, 21, 23 (top), 24, 26, 28, 30 (bottom), 30, 31 (top); Richard Morden, pp. 8, 9, 12, 13, 14,
15, 17, 18, 22, 23 (bottom), 27, 29, 31 (bottom); Karen Young, p. 1 and Try This! logo.
Production Controller: Vanessa Johnson

Printed in China

Acknowledgements

The author and the publisher are grateful to the following for permission to reproduce copyright material:

Front cover photograph:
Roller coaster, © Dave Raboin/iStockphoto; Spinning top, © Ruta Saulyte-Laurinaviciene/Shutterstock; Kite, © Grafissimo/
iStockphoto.

Photos courtesy of:
Jeremy Horner/Getty Images, **10**; © dwphotos/iStockphoto, **8** (left); © Grafissimo/iStockphoto, **28** © Lee Foster/
iStockphoto, **25** (bottom); © Sven Klaschik/iStockphoto, **4**; © Ann Marie Kurtz/iStockphoto, **14**; © Milos Luzanin/
iStockphoto, **20** (left); © ranplett/iStockphoto, **11** (top); © Craig Veltri/iStockphoto, **25** (top); Jupiter Unlimited, **11** (bottom);
Photolibrary, **19** (bottom); © Anthony Harris/Shutterstock, **5**; © Jonathan Larsen/Shutterstock, **19** (top); © Ruta Saulyte-
Laurinaviciene/Shutterstock, **19** (middle); © Monkey Business Images/Shutterstock, **20** (right).

Activity adapted from www.pbs.org/benfranklin/exp_kite.html, **29**.

While every care has been taken to trace and acknowledge copyright, the publisher tenders their apologies for any
accidental infringement where copyright has proved untraceable. Where the attempt has been unsuccessful, the publisher
welcomes information that would redress the situation.

The publisher would like to thank Heidi Ruhnau, Head of Science at Oxley College, for her assistance in reviewing
manuscripts.

Please note
At the time of printing, the Internet addresses appearing in this book were correct. Owing to the dynamic nature of the
Internet, however, we cannot guarantee that all these addresses will remain correct.

▶ Contents

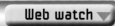

Look out for these features throughout the book:

'Word watch' explains the meanings of words shown in **bold**

Web watch ▼

'Web watch' provides website suggestions for further research

Understanding our world through science

Science = knowledge

The word 'science' comes from the Latin word *scientia,* which means 'knowledge'.

▲ Humans look at the things around them and ask 'Why?' and 'How?'. Science helps answer these questions.

Science is amazing! Through science, we can understand more about our world and ourselves. Without science, we would not have a clue – about anything!

Shared knowledge

Science exists because humans are curious. We are curious about how things work, about the Earth and its place in the universe, about life and survival, about the natural world around us and about time, space and speed. We are curious about everything! We never stop asking questions.

Science is the knowledge that humans have gathered about the physical and natural world and how it works. This knowledge is gathered through **experimentation** and **observation**.

Word watch

experimentation using scientific procedures to make discoveries, test ideas and prove facts

observation watching carefully in order to gain information

The science behind theme parks, playgrounds and toys

Theme parks, playgrounds and toys are lots of fun. They also teach us a lot about the branch of science called physics.

What is physics?

Physics is the study of the way things act, the way they react with each other and the way they move. A more scientific description is that physics is the study of matter and energy. Matter is anything that occupies space. Gases, liquids and solid objects are all matter. Energy brings about **motion** and **force**.

We use physics to explain how things work. Physics helps to explain what the universe is made of, how the universe began and how things in the universe act. It helps to explain how a light globe works and how heavy aeroplanes can move through the air without crashing to the ground. Physics also helps to explain how theme park rides, playground equipment and toys work.

▶ The science of physics explains how a kite can fly.

The scientists behind the science

There are many different branches of physics. Scientists who study physics are called physicists.

Scientist and area of study

Astrophysicist The universe and the matter that exists within the universe

Biophysicist How physics works within living organisms

Fluid physicist The physics of fluids (liquids and gases)

Geophysicists The physics of the Earth

Nuclear physicist The way atoms act and react

Optical physicist The properties and movement of light

Word watch

force a push or a pull
motion movement

5

How do roller-coasters work?

Roller-coasters do not have engines. They depend on several key elements of physics to work, including energy, **gravity** and **friction**. Understanding how a roller-coaster works also requires an understanding of Newton's first law of **motion**.

Roller-coasters and energy, gravity and friction

There are two types of energy, potential energy and **kinetic energy**, and roller-coasters use both types. Potential energy is stored energy, while kinetic energy is the energy of movement. At the top of a roller-coaster's first hill, its cars have a certain amount of potential energy, which is converted to kinetic energy as soon as the cars are released. The higher the hill, the more kinetic energy the cars have when they are released.

Newton's first law of motion states that an object stays at rest or it will continue in unchanging motion in a straight line unless it is acted on by an external **force**. This law applies to all objects, including roller-coasters.

Gravity is the force that pulls all objects toward the centre of the Earth. As the roller-coaster rushes down the hill, gravity converts the potential energy to kinetic energy, speeding up the ride. Friction occurs between the roller-coaster cars and the tracks, as well as between the cars and the air, slowing the roller-coaster down.

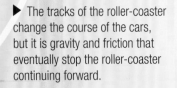

▶ The tracks of the roller-coaster change the course of the cars, but it is gravity and friction that eventually stop the roller-coaster continuing forward.

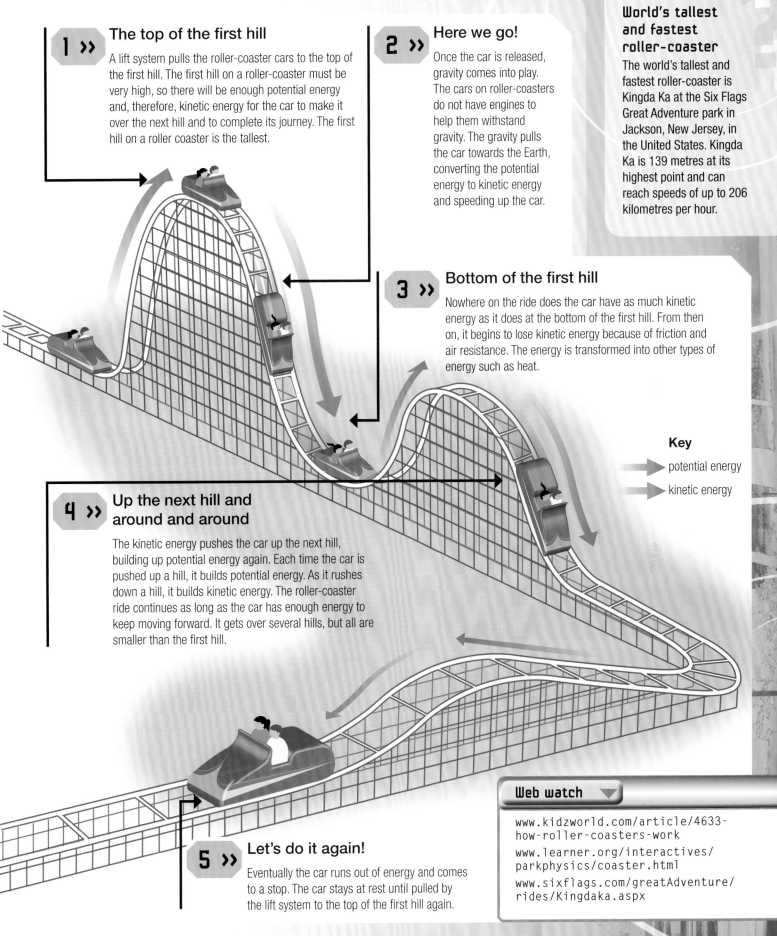

1 » The top of the first hill

A lift system pulls the roller-coaster cars to the top of the first hill. The first hill on a roller-coaster must be very high, so there will be enough potential energy and, therefore, kinetic energy for the car to make it over the next hill and to complete its journey. The first hill on a roller coaster is the tallest.

2 » Here we go!

Once the car is released, gravity comes into play. The cars on roller-coasters do not have engines to help them withstand gravity. The gravity pulls the car towards the Earth, converting the potential energy to kinetic energy and speeding up the car.

World's tallest and fastest roller-coaster

The world's tallest and fastest roller-coaster is Kingda Ka at the Six Flags Great Adventure park in Jackson, New Jersey, in the United States. Kingda Ka is 139 metres at its highest point and can reach speeds of up to 206 kilometres per hour.

3 » Bottom of the first hill

Nowhere on the ride does the car have as much kinetic energy as it does at the bottom of the first hill. From then on, it begins to lose kinetic energy because of friction and air resistance. The energy is transformed into other types of energy such as heat.

Key

→ potential energy

→ kinetic energy

4 » Up the next hill and around and around

The kinetic energy pushes the car up the next hill, building up potential energy again. Each time the car is pushed up a hill, it builds potential energy. As it rushes down a hill, it builds kinetic energy. The roller-coaster ride continues as long as the car has enough energy to keep moving forward. It gets over several hills, but all are smaller than the first hill.

5 » Let's do it again!

Eventually the car runs out of energy and comes to a stop. The car stays at rest until pulled by the lift system to the top of the first hill again.

Web watch ▼

www.kidzworld.com/article/4633-how-roller-coasters-work

www.learner.org/interactives/parkphysics/coaster.html

www.sixflags.com/greatAdventure/rides/Kingdaka.aspx

Why do I move forward when my bumper car is hit from the front?

The reason why your body continues to move forward when your bumper car is hit from the front has to do with Newton's first law of **motion**. Bumper car rides also provide an opportunity to see how Newton's other two laws of motion work.

Newton's first law of motion

Newton's first law of motion states that an object stays at rest or it will continue in a state of unchanging motion in a straight line unless it is acted on by an external **force**. When your bumper car is hit from the front by another bumper car, your car's forward **momentum** is stopped. As a result, your car stops or is forced to change direction.

Newton's first law of motion also explains why you keep moving forward when this happens. Your body's forward motion has not been stopped, so your body continues to move in the same direction it was moving before the bump. Only when an outside force, such as your seatbelt, stops this momentum do you stop moving forward. This is why you have to wear a seatbelt on bumper car rides. Without it, you would be thrown out of the car every time you hit another car.

▲ At an amusement park, drivers of bumper cars race and try to knock each other out of the way.

Word watch

force a push or a pull
momentum amount of motion of a moving body
motion movement

► When two bumper cars collide, the drivers' bodies keep moving forward until they are stopped by their seatbelts.

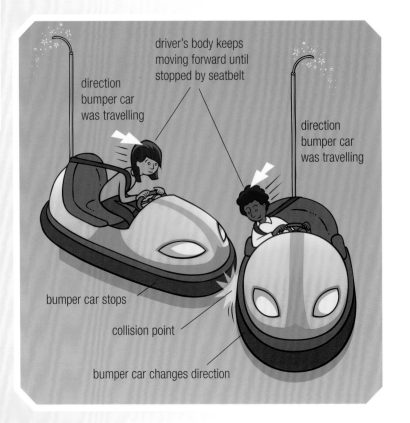

direction bumper car was travelling

driver's body keeps moving forward until stopped by seatbelt

direction bumper car was travelling

bumper car stops

collision point

bumper car changes direction

Newton's second law of motion

Newton's second law of motion states that the amount of force needed to make an object change its speed depends on the **mass** of the object. This means that the heavier something is, the harder it is to stop. So, if an adult runs towards you, the best thing for you to do is get out of their way. It would be very hard for you to stop them. If a small child runs towards you, however, it should be easier for you to stop them.

In the case of bumper cars, Newton's second law of motion relates to the drivers rather than the cars, which are all usually the same size. The less mass a driver has, the more likely they are to be jolted about when hit. The heavier a driver is, the harder it is to move them around, so the less they are jolted when hit.

Newton's third law of motion

Newton's third law of motion states that for every action, there is an equal and opposite reaction. If two bumper cars travelling at the same speed and carrying the same amount of mass hit each other, they will both bounce back and come to a stop the same distance away from their collision point. This assumes that no other outside force, such as another bumper car or a wall, comes into contact with one of the bumper cars.

driver's body keeps moving forward until stopped by seatbelt

driver's body keeps moving forward until stopped by seatbelt

direction bumper car was travelling

direction bumper car was travelling

bumper car stops

bumper car stops

▲ When two bumper cars collide, a lighter driver will be jolted about more than a heavier driver.

▶ If two bumper cars with equally weighted drivers collide while travelling the same speed, they will bounce back the same distance.

collision point

Web watch

www.learner.org/interactives/parkphysics/bumpcars.html

9

Why do I look so silly in fairground mirrors?

Your appearance in a fairground mirror looks strange because the mirror is not flat. The mirror curves both in and out. As a result, light bounces off the mirror at different angles, forming strange kinds of reflections.

How light travels

Light travels in a continuous straight line until it hits something that causes it to detour from this path. Light passes directly through glass and air. When light passes from air into water, however, its path bends. This effect is known as refraction.

When light hits a mirror, it does not pass through it. It bounces back. The direction that the light bounces back depends on the surface of the mirror.

Flat mirrors

Light is **reflected** when it hits a mirror. If the mirror has a completely flat surface, all the reflected light is reflected back in the same direction, creating a mirror image. A mirror image shows the objects in front of the mirror at the same size but in reverse.

Most bathroom mirrors and mirrors in clothes shops are flat mirrors. Flat mirrors are also known as plane mirrors.

◀ When light hits a fairground mirror, it bounces back in many directions. This causes a strange reflection.

Convex mirrors

A convex mirror is a mirror that bulges outwards. When light hits a convex mirror, the reflected light spreads out. The image in the mirror appears smaller than normal.

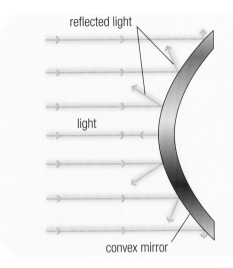

▲ The light that is reflected from a convex mirror is spread out.

▲ Convex mirrors are used as rear view mirrors in cars, because they pick up a lot of the background.

Try this!

Look into a spoon with the ladle side facing away from you. The back of the spoon is a convex surface, so the image of your face will appear small and you will be able to see a lot of the background behind you.

Now, look into a spoon with the ladle side facing towards you. This is a concave surface. The image of your face will appear upside down.

Concave mirrors

A concave mirror is a mirror that bulges inwards. When light hits a concave mirror, the light is directed inwards to one focal point. The image that can be seen in the mirror depends on the distance between the viewer and the mirror. At a certain distance, the light rays cross over and spread out, causing the image to appear upside down.

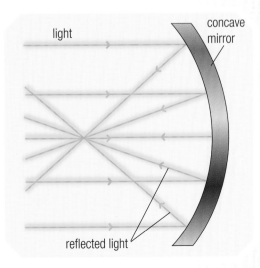

▲ The light that is reflected from a concave mirror is focused inwards.

▲ Concave mirrors are used as shaving mirrors, because objects look larger than normal.

Do heavier people go down slides faster than lighter people?

Many things affect how fast someone goes down a slide, such as the angle of the slide, the clothes that the person is wearing and what the slide is made from. If all these things are the same, however, a heavier person will go down a slide slower than a lighter person, because of **friction**.

The effect of friction

Friction slows or stops objects sliding past each other. Smooth or greasy surfaces have less friction than bumpy or rough surfaces.

Mass also has an effect on the degree, or level, of friction. Heavier things create more friction when they are moving, so a heavier person will go down a slide slower than a lighter person.

Reducing friction

Oil and grease are often used to reduce friction. Machines and cars are greased and oiled to prevent their many moving parts rubbing against each other and causing damage. If you wipe oil along a slide before using it, you will slide faster.

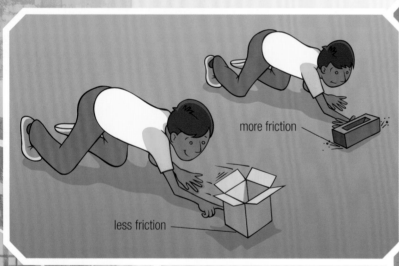

more friction

less friction

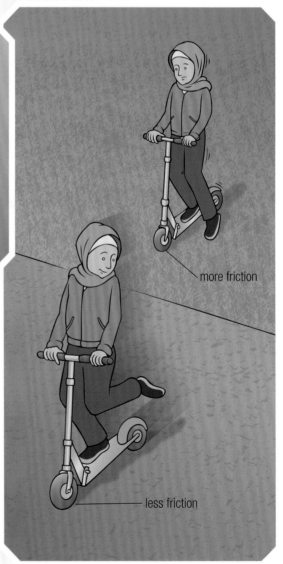

more friction

less friction

Word watch

friction force that resists motion and slows an object

mass amount of matter in an object, which is similar but not identical to the weight of an object

Web watch ▼

www.mrfizzix. com/playground/ page_2.htm

▲ Try pushing a heavy brick across a cement surface. Now try pushing an empty box of similar size across the same surface. The box is a lot easier to push. Part of this is because the box has fewer rough edges than the brick, but mostly this is because the box is lighter than the brick.

▶ Try riding a scooter across grass. Now try riding the same scooter across a cement surface. It is far easier to ride across the cement surface because there is less friction between the wheels of the scooter and the cement than there is between the wheels of the scooter and the grass.

The effect of gravity

The speed at which a person travels down a slide also depends on the steepness of the slide. The steeper the slide, the greater the effect of **gravity** and the faster the person travels.

Slides work because of gravity. Gravity is the **force** that draws objects towards the centre of the Earth. When you sit at the top of a slide, before sliding down, the only thing that stops you from falling to the ground is the structure that you are sitting on. Once you move your body onto the **inclined plane**, you no longer have the same level of support and gravity forces you downwards. If there was no inclined plane and you were falling freely, without any air resistance, you would accelerate at 9.8 metres per second each second.

Because you are on a slide, you do not reach the same acceleration as if you were free-falling. This is because part of the force of gravity presses you to the slide, leaving only part of it to pull you towards the ground.

▶ A heavy person will slide more slowly down a slide than a lighter person.

heavy person   lighter person

▲ A heavy person will free-fall to the ground at the same acceleration as a lighter person. Every object free-falls at the same rate of change of speed, no matter how much its mass is, except when air resistance has an effect (for example, feathers floating).

Try this!

If you rub your hand rapidly backwards and forwards across the top of a table or desk, you can feel your hand warming up. This is like sliding down a slide: the kinetic energy is being converted into heat.

Slides and energy

When you sit at the top of a slide, you have potential energy. When you start sliding, the potential energy is converted into **kinetic energy** (see page 6). Friction acts to convert this kinetic energy into **thermal energy**. This is why parts of your body that are in contact with a slide sometimes heat up as you slide down.

Word watch

force a push or a pull

gravity force that pulls objects towards one another

inclined plane flat surface on a lean or a slope

kinetic energy energy of an object in motion

thermal energy heat energy

Why does moving my legs help me swing higher?

A swing is a **pendulum**. It swings you and the seat high into the air. You can swing higher and longer by moving your legs backwards and forwards.

Move those legs!

Moving your legs on a swing helps the swing increase its height. It is not really the action of your legs that causes this, but the shifting of your body as you kick. By moving your body you are moving your centre of **gravity** and this provides you with more **momentum**.

Word watch

friction force that resists motion and slows an object

gravity force that pulls objects towards one another

kinetic energy energy of a body in motion

momentum amount of motion of a moving body

observations information that is gained by watching something carefully

pendulum weighted piece of wire, rope or other material that swings at a regular rate

▲ A girl kicks her legs so she swings higher and longer.

How a pendulum works

A pendulum relies on gravity to function. Once a pendulum is given a push, it continues swinging backwards and forwards until all its **kinetic energy** is converted to other types of energy due to **friction** and air resistance.

When it runs out of kinetic energy, the pendulum or the swing needs to be pushed again to gain more momentum. The weight of the object that is suspended on the pendulum does not influence how fast the pendulum swings.

Web watch ▼

www.mrfizzix.com/
playground/page_5.htm

Point A

Point B

Point A

Point B

◀ A swing will take the same length of time to get from Point A to Point B, whether it is holding a child who weighs 30 kilograms or an adult who weighs 90 kilograms.

14

Potential energy and kinetic energy

Like a roller-coaster (pages 6–7) and slide (pages 12–13), swings show how potential energy is converted to **kinetic energy** and how kinetic energy is converted to potential energy.

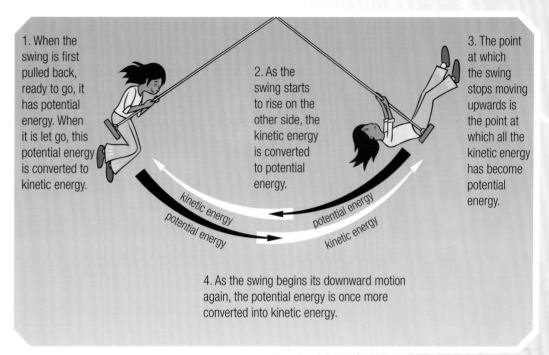

1. When the swing is first pulled back, ready to go, it has potential energy. When it is let go, this potential energy is converted to kinetic energy.

2. As the swing starts to rise on the other side, the kinetic energy is converted to potential energy.

3. The point at which the swing stops moving upwards is the point at which all the kinetic energy has become potential energy.

kinetic energy
potential energy
potential energy
kinetic energy

4. As the swing begins its downward motion again, the potential energy is once more converted into kinetic energy.

▲ The process of converting potential energy to kinetic energy and back again continues as the swing moves backwards and forwards.

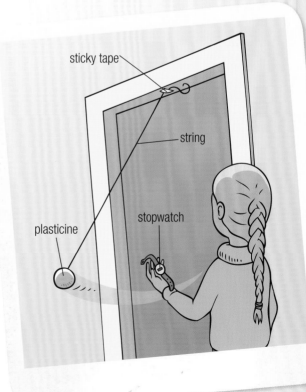

sticky tape

string

plasticine

stopwatch

Try this!

Make a pendulum

This simple experiment will show you how a pendulum works.

1. Attach a blob of plasticine to one end of a one-metre-long piece of string.

2. Using the sticky tape, tape the other end of the string to the top of a doorframe.

3. Pull the plasticine all the way back and let go.

4. Time how long it takes for the pendulum to complete ten swings.

5. Add more to the blob to make it heavier.

6. Repeat the swinging and timing process. The pendulum will take the same amount of time to swing ten times, no matter how heavy the blob.

How can two people of different weight make a seesaw stay level?

If two people of the same weight sit on each end of a seesaw, the seesaw is balanced and can be made level. It is also possible to make a seesaw level if the two people are of very different weights.

Levers

A seesaw is an example of a lever. A lever is a device that has a **fulcrum** about which the lever turns or is supported. Levers are designed to make it easier to lift heavy objects. When effort is applied to one part of the lever, a **load** is lifted with the help of the fulcrum.

There are three types of levers. They differ according to the position of the fulcrum, effort and load.

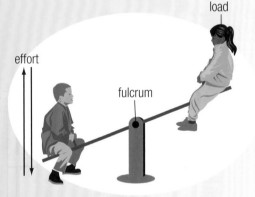

First class levers

These levers have the effort on one side of the fulcrum and the load on the other side of the fulcrum.

◀ A seesaw is an example of a first class lever.

Second class levers

These levers have the fulcrum at one end, the effort at the other end and the load in the middle.

◀ A wheelbarrow is an example of a second class lever.

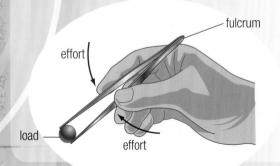

Third class levers

These levers have the fulcrum at one end, the load at the other end and the effort in the middle.

◀ A pair of tweezers is an example of a third class lever.

Balancing a seesaw

To balance two differently weighted people on a seesaw, each person's **newtons** (N) needs to be calculated. A newton measures **force**. Each person's newton measurement decides where they should be positioned on each side of the fulcrum. A seesaw is balanced when one person's newtons (N) multiplied by their distance from the fulcrum equals the other person's newtons multiplied by their distance from the fulcrum.

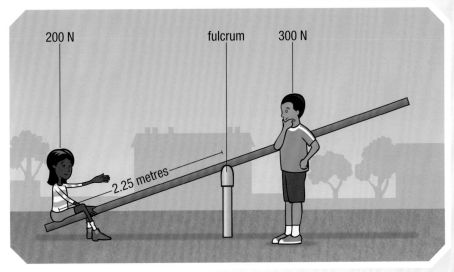

▲ Jessica's newtons equal 200 and she is sitting 2.25 metres from the fulcrum. Lee's newtons equal 300. Where should Lee sit for the seesaw to be balanced?

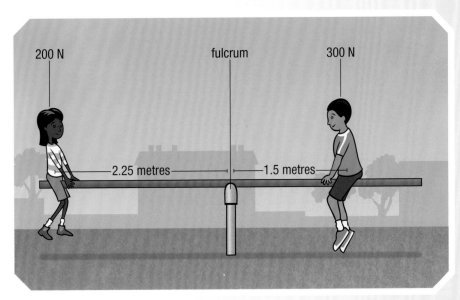

▲ Jessica's newtons (200) multiplied by her distance from the fulcrum (2.25 metres) is 450. Knowing this, we can calculate where Lee should sit. By dividing 450 by Lee's newtons (300), we get 1.5. Lee should sit 1.5 metres from the fulcrum for the seesaw to balance.

force a push or a pull

newtons units of measurement of force

mass amount of matter in an object, which is similar but not identical to the weight of an object

Web watch ▼

www.mrfizzix.com/playground/page_3.htm

Why does a spinning top keep turning around?

If you stand a top on its end and let it go, it will just fall over. If you start spinning the top, however, it should keep spinning and stay upright for a long time. This is due to **momentum**.

Understanding momentum

Some objects with momentum are hard to stop. Think of a bicycle, a car and a truck travelling down a road. They all have momentum, but the larger the object is and the faster it goes, the more momentum it has. The more momentum it has, the harder it is to stop. This type of momentum is called **linear** momentum because the objects are moving in a straight line.

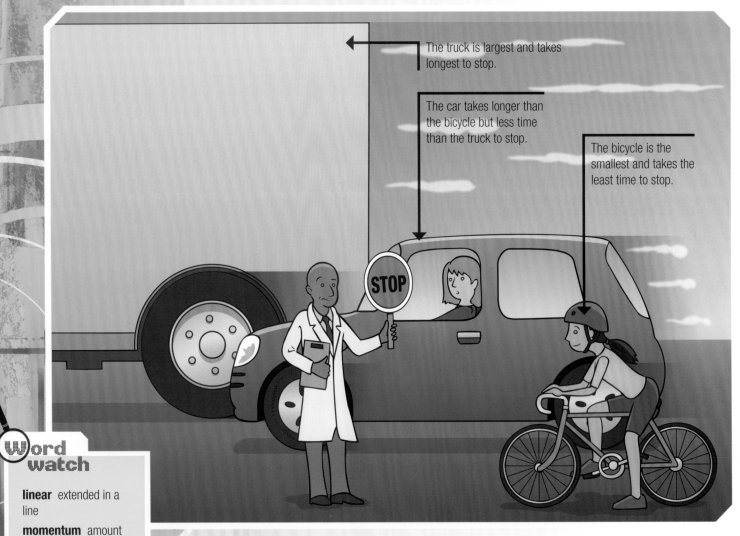

The truck is largest and takes longest to stop.

The car takes longer than the bicycle but less time than the truck to stop.

The bicycle is the smallest and takes the least time to stop.

STOP

▲ If they are all travelling the same speed, it is harder to stop a moving car than it is to stop a moving bicycle, and it is harder to stop a moving truck than a moving car.

Understanding angular momentum

Angular momentum is movement around a point, like the way a top spins around on its point. Just as it is hard to stop a large object with large linear momentum, it is hard to stop a large object with a lot of angular momentum.

A spinning object, such as a top, would continue spinning forever if there was nothing to stop it. This follows Newton's first law of **motion** that states that an object stays at rest or in a state of uniform motion in a straight line unless acted on by an external force (see pages 6 and 8).

One thing that slows down objects with angular momentum is **friction**. Touching a spinning top on its side will cause friction, which will slow it down, just as friction slows down a person on a slide (see page 12).

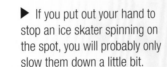

▶ If you put out your hand to stop an ice skater spinning on the spot, you will probably only slow them down a little bit.

▲ Touching a spinning top will slow or stop its motion.

▲ It is easy to stop a small coin that is spinning around and around.

Angular momentum in the solar system

Large objects that use angular momentum are the Earth, the Moon and the planets. The Earth spins around on its **axis** while it orbits the Sun.

Word watch

angular at an angle

axis imaginary line around which something, such as the Earth, spins

friction force that resists motion and slows an object

motion movement

Web watch ▼

www.spintastics.com/HistoryofTop.asp

How do yoyos come back up?

The aim of playing with a yoyo is to get the yoyo to keep coming back up the string, eventually returning to your hand. Yoyos use **angular momentum**, but they also rise up and fall down because of **gravity** and energy.

Yoyos and gravity

A person playing with a yoyo holds the end of the string and drops the yoyo. Gravity makes the yoyo fall to the ground. Each time the yoyo climbs back up the string, gravity makes it fall again. This process continues until the energy that allows the yoyo to climb back up the string is converted to other types of energy, such as heat.

▶ A boy tries to keep the yoyo moving up and down the string for as long as possible.

▼ A yoyo has three main parts: the string, the axle and the case.

piece of string

axle

end of the string is looped around the axle

outside case

Yoyos and energy

When you hold a yoyo in your hand before you release it, it has potential energy. Potential energy is stored energy. As soon as you release the yoyo, the potential energy is converted into **kinetic energy**. As the yoyo goes down and up the string, potential energy changes to kinetic energy and back again. This is similar to what happens with a roller-coaster (page 6) and a swing (page 15).

Friction and air resistance eventually cause this energy to be converted to other types of energy and the up and down **motion** to stop. Gravity forces the yoyo to the bottom of the string where it comes to a stop. Before this happens, the person with the yoyo may catch it in their hand, which is another form of resistance.

Yoyos and momentum

A spinning yoyo has both **linear** and angular momentum (see page 18). Linear momentum keeps the yoyo moving up and down the string. Angular momentum keeps the yoyo spinning around as the yoyo moves up and down.

All objects fall at the same acceleration towards the Earth (see page 13), but if you let go of a spinning yoyo and another object at the same time and from the same height, the other object would hit the ground first. This is because angular momentum slows the yoyo down.

As the yoyo starts climbing up the string, the kinetic energy is gradually converted back to potential energy.

At the bottom of the string, almost all the energy is kinetic energy

Key

→ potential energy
→ kinetic energy

▲ As the yoyo goes up and down, the energy changes forms.

angular momentum (spinning of yoyo)

▲ Angular momentum slows the fall of the yoyo, and the coin falls more quickly.

First toy in space
The yoyo was the first toy in space. The crew of the space shuttle *Discovery* took a yoyo on their 1985 mission.

Yoyos in history
The ancient Greeks played with yoyos about 2500 years ago. The Chinese may have had yoyos even earlier. It is thought that the yoyo was used as a weapon in the Philippines.

Word watch

friction force that resists motion and slows an object

kinetic energy energy of an object in motion

linear extended in a line

motion movement

Why are bubbles always round?

Even if you blow a bubble through a square bubble blower, the bubble will be round! Nature often tries to do things in the easiest possible way and a **sphere** requires less effort to form than any other shape.

Properties of a sphere

All points on a sphere are an equal distance from the centre. This makes spheres **economical**. When a bubble is formed, no part of the liquid has to travel further than any other part of the liquid. Spheres also have less surface area for the volume that is inside them than any other shape.

A sphere is **three-dimensional**. A circle is like a sphere, but it is only **two-dimensional**.

Try this! ## Measure a circle

Follow this simple experiment and discover how circles are like spheres.

Materials

⤺ Paper ⤺ Pencil ⤺ Protractor

Steps

1. Draw a circle using the protractor.

2. Find the centre of the circle and make a mark.

3. Using the measurement marks on the protractor, measure the distance from the centre to several different points on the edge of the circle.

4. Use the straight end of the protractor to draw other shapes, such as a square, rectangle and triangle.

5. Find the centre of each shape and measure to several points on its edges.

Observation

Only with the circle will you find that the distance from the centre to any point on the edge is the same.

Surface tension

Bubbles are able to form because of surface tension. Surface tension is a **force** that pulls the molecules on the surface of a liquid towards the **molecules** next to them and beneath them.

A bubble is made from a very thin layer of water mixed with detergent. Molecules of detergent have parts that **bind** to water and other parts that **repel** water. When detergent is added to water, the parts that bind to water squeeze between the water molecules and reduce the surface tension between them. The parts that repel from water stick out from the surface.

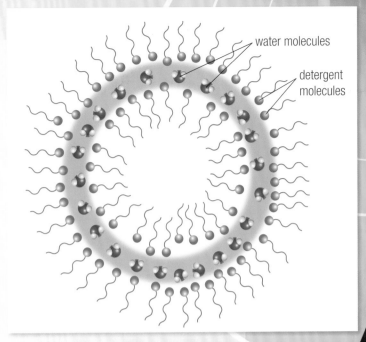
water molecules
detergent molecules

▲ A bubble's surface is a combination of water molecules and detergent molecules. As you blow a bubble, the water and detergent mixture spreads out to make a thin layer in the shape of a sphere, because the surface tension between the molecules is no longer strong enough to pull them tightly together.

Word watch

bind fasten tightly
force a push or a pull
molecules groups of atoms joined together
repel drive or force away

Try this!

Make bubbles

In this experiment, you will test if it is possible to blow bubbles in shapes other than a sphere.

Materials

⊃ Bubble mixture
⊃ Pipe cleaners

Steps

1. Make a round bubble blower out of a pipe cleaner. Dip the bubble blower in the mixture and blow a bubble.

2. Now, make a square bubble blower, an oblong bubble blower and a triangular bubble blower. Dip these bubble blowers in the mixture and blow bubbles.

3. Now, make some three-dimensional bubble blowers, such as a triangular prism and a cube. Dip these bubble blowers in the mixture and blow bubbles.

Observation

No matter what shape the bubble blowers are, the bubbles will always be spheres.

Web watch

ksnn.larc.nasa.gov/
webtext.cfm?unit=bubbles
www.exploratorium.edu/
ronh/bubbles/bubbles.html

How do remote control toys receive their signals?

Popular remote control toys are cars, planes, boats and robots. The signals that tell these toys where to go and how fast to move are transferred through the air in invisible waves.

Radio signals

Radio signals travel through the air in waves. These waves are part of the electromagnetic spectrum.

Radio signals carry information such as images and data. A radio transmitter is used to create radio waves in different ways, such as by creating electrical **pulses** at a certain **frequency**. The frequency is the number of waves that pass a point each second. It is measured in units called hertz (Hz), with one hertz equal to one wave per second.

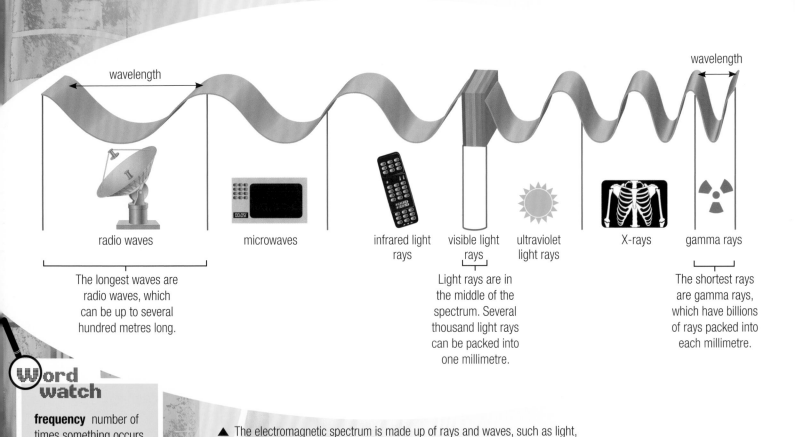

wavelength

wavelength

radio waves | microwaves | infrared light rays | visible light rays | ultraviolet light rays | X-rays | gamma rays

The longest waves are radio waves, which can be up to several hundred metres long.

Light rays are in the middle of the spectrum. Several thousand light rays can be packed into one millimetre.

The shortest rays are gamma rays, which have billions of rays packed into each millimetre.

▲ The electromagnetic spectrum is made up of rays and waves, such as light, heat radiation, X-rays, microwaves and radio waves. These rays and waves are arranged by wavelength, from longest to shortest.

How remote control toys work

Remote control toys work when radio signals are sent from a transmitter, which is held by the person controlling the toy, to a receiver, which is inside the toy.

1 » The control is held by the person controlling the toy. When the control is moved in different ways, different **sequences** of electrical pulses are created. These electrical pulses make up the signal that is to be sent.

2 » The transmitter sends out the radio signal to the receiver. Both the transmitter and the receiver have been set up to only receive signals at a particular frequency.

3 » Once the receiver receives the signal, it decodes it. The receiver knows what each different sequence of pulses means. It counts the number of electrical pulses in the signal and directs the motor to move in a certain way.

None of these steps would work without a power source. The power source may be a rechargeable battery or a normal battery.

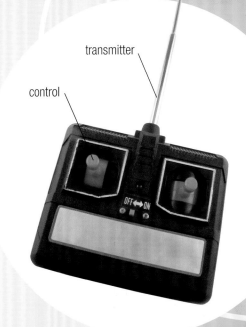

transmitter

control

Word **watch**

sequences series of items that follow each other in a particular order

power source

receiver

motor

▲ Remote control toys need five main components to work. They need a control, transmitter, receiver, motor and power source.

Web watch ▼

www.rc-wiki.com/
wiki/Radio_control

Why do super balls bounce so high?

When you drop a super ball to the ground, it will bounce back almost to the height from which you dropped it. Normal balls do not do this. A super ball will also continue bouncing for longer than normal balls.

Balls and energy

When you hold any type of ball in your hand, the ball has potential energy. Potential energy is stored energy. When you drop the ball, the potential energy is converted to **kinetic energy**.

When the ball hits the ground, **friction** converts some of the kinetic energy into another form of energy, **thermal energy**. Thermal energy is heat. If friction did not reduce the amount of kinetic energy like this, the ball would continue bouncing forever.

Super balls and energy

Super balls are made from different types of rubber. Rubber has **elastic** properties. This elasticity reduces the amount of friction that occurs when the ball hits the ground. This means that a super ball can bounce higher and longer than balls made from other materials. It retains its kinetic energy for longer.

The Super Bowl
The Super Bowl, a championship game in the American National Football League, was named after the super ball. An owner of one of the football teams watched his children play with a super ball and decided that Super Bowl would be a good name for the yearly game.

Word watch

elastic able to go back to its original shape after being stretched or compressed

friction force that resists motion and slows an object

kinetic energy energy of an object in motion

thermal energy heat energy

▶ A super ball is made from rubber. The rubber's elasticity means the super ball can keep its kinetic energy for longer and bounce higher and longer than other balls.

Make a super ball

Follow this simple experiment to make your own super ball.

Materials

- Plastic garbage bag
- Jug
- Glass of water
- Woodwork glue
- 2 small spoonfuls of borax (a type of laundry detergent)
- Bowl
- Food colouring

Steps

1. Cover a table with the plastic garbage bag. This is to protect the table.

2. Pour a glass of water into the jug. Add the borax and stir to dissolve.

3. Squirt some glue into a bowl. Add a dash of food colouring and stir.

4. Add the dissolved borax to the mixture in the bowl.

5. Stir until the mixture gets thick. Then, add a bit more water.

6. Pour the mixture onto the plastic bag. Leave it to dry for a few minutes.

7. Roll the mixture into a ball.

8. Bounce the ball!

Observation

When you bounce the ball, it should bounce high like a super ball. The glue provides the ball with its bounce, while the borax keeps the ball in the right shape. The food colouring gives the ball its colour.

Inventing the super ball

American chemist Norman Stingley invented the super ball in 1965. Just for fun, he compressed a synthetic rubber material under a lot of pressure to see what would happen. He created a very bouncy ball. A company began to make these 'Super Balls', which became very popular all over the world.

Ask a parent or carer to help you with this experiment. They can help you prepare the mixture safely.

Web watch

van.physics.illinois. edu/qa/listing. php?id=101

www.superballs.com/

How do kites stay up?

If you throw a kite into the air, it will fall down to the ground like any other object. It is heavier than the air. If you have thrust and lift, however, you can fly your kite all day long.

Newton's third law of motion

The scientist Isaac Newton (1642–1727) spent a great deal of time looking at **force** and **motion**. His third law of motion helps to explain how kites fly. This law states that for every action there is an equal and opposite reaction. In the case of a kite, **gravity** and drag are balanced out by lift and thrust.

Gravity and lift

Lift occurs when wind passes over the body of the kite, moves underneath it and lifts the kite into the air. Lift operates at a 90-degree angle to the direction of the wind, so it directly opposes gravity, which pulls things towards the Earth.

When the wind drops, the amount of lift also drops and gravity forces the kite downwards. This is why you cannot fly a kite when there is no wind.

Drag and thrust

The other two forces that oppose each other are thrust and drag. Thrust is generated by pulling on the string that is attached to the kite's body. This thrust helps the kite stay in the air. Drag is the air **friction** that occurs as the kite flies through the air.

▲ The design of kites allows them to fly.

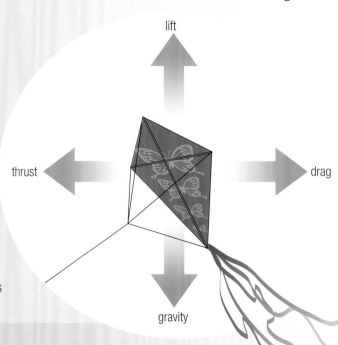

▶ To fly, a kite needs four forces acting on it.

lift

thrust

drag

gravity

Make a kite

Follow this simple activity and make your own kite.

Materials

- 60-centimetre lightweight stick
- 50-centimetre lightweight stick
- Heavy-duty garbage bag
- Masking tape
- Lightweight string or twine
- Craft knife
- Ruler
- Pencil, pen or marker
- Scissors
- Ribbon

Steps

1. With the help of an adult, use the craft knife to carve a notch into each end of the sticks.

2. Using a ruler, mark a spot on the longer stick 15 centimetres from one end. Mark a spot in the middle of the smaller stick, 25 centimetres from each end.

3. Cross the shorter stick over the longer stick, matching up the marks. Make sure all the notches are parallel to the ground.

4. Take the string and wrap it around the centre of the sticks.

5. Thread the string through all the notches, creating a diamond shape. Wrap it around twice, making sure the string is tight. This is the frame of your kite.

6. Wrap the end of the string tightly around both sticks again. Tie it off with a knot.

7. Cut the plastic bag so that it is slightly larger than the frame. Fold the bag over the frame. Tape or glue it down.

9. Reinforce the top and bottom tips of the kite with tape. Use a pen or scissors to punch a tiny hole through these reinforced tips.

10. Cut a 25-centimetre piece of string. Knot one end of the string through the top hole and the other end through the bottom hole. This is the bridle.

11. Tape or knot 150 centimetres of string to the bottom tip of your kite. Tie ribbons around the string. This is the tail of the kite.

12. Take the remainder of your string. Attach one end to the bridle, about one-third of the way down. This is the flying string.

13. Wait for a windy day and start flying!

Source: Activity adapted from www.pbs.org/benfranklin/exp_kite.html

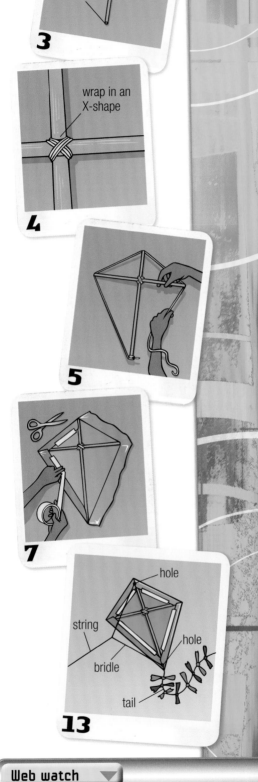

3 notches

4 wrap in an X-shape

5

7

13 hole / string / bridle / hole / tail

Web watch ▼

www.gombergkites.com/nkm/why.html
www.ehow.com/how_1289_fly-kite.html

How do magnets work?

Many toys are made from magnets or use magnets to work. Magnets have the ability to **attract** and **repel** some metals. They do so using a **force** known as magnetism.

Magnetic metals

Magnets are made from a particular metal or metals. Magnetite is a metal that is a natural magnet. Some other metals that contain magnetic qualities are iron, steel, nickel and cobalt. This means that these metals can be turned into magnets.

Everything is made up of **atoms**. Inside these atoms are particles called electrons, which spin around the atoms and cause them to move. If the atoms in an object line up and move in the same direction, a strong magnetic force is created. This can happen in metals with magnetic qualities.

Magnetic fields

A magnetic field is an area around a magnet. Inside this area, other metal items are attracted to the magnet. Outside this area, a magnet's force has no effect.

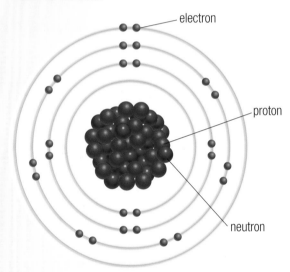

▲ Electrons spin around an iron atom.

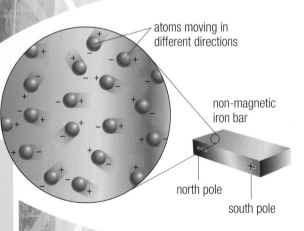

▲ Iron atoms usually move in different directions so a piece of iron is not usually magnetic. If a piece of iron is placed near a magnet, however, its atoms line up. This makes the iron magnetic.

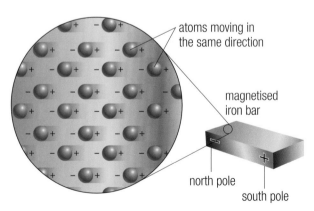

Magnetic poles

All magnets have a north pole and a south pole. Unlike poles attract and like poles repel. In other words, the north pole of one magnet and the south pole of another magnet will attract each other, but two north poles or two south poles will repel each other.

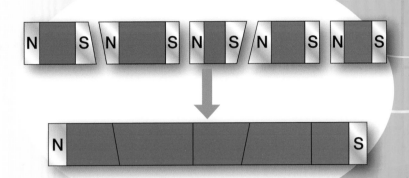

▲ Putting a north pole next to a south pole, next to a north pole, next to a south pole will create one long magnet.

Try this!

Make a magnet

This experiment turns an ordinary nail into a magnet.

Materials

⮑ Magnet   ⮑ Iron nail   ⮑ Some paper clips

Steps

1. Try to pick up the paper clips with the nail.

2. Now, stroke the nail about 50 times against one end of the magnet. Use the same end of the magnet and always stroke in the same direction.

3. Try again to pick up the paper clips with the nail. The nail should now work as a magnet.

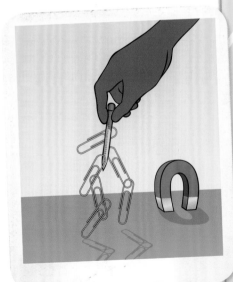

Observation

The nail has been turned into a magnet, because the force from the original magnet has made all the nail's atoms face the same direction.

The Earth is a magnet

Movement within the core of the Earth creates a magnetic force. The Earth's poles are known as the north magnetic pole and the south magnetic pole.

Web watch ▼

www.education.com/ reference/article/ Ref_Magnets_Gravity/

Index